EXTREME ENGINEERING

CHANNEL TUNNEL

BY ASHLEY GISH

WWW.APEXEDITIONS.COM

Copyright © 2024 by Apex Editions, Mendota Heights, MN 55120. All rights reserved. No part of this book may be reproduced or utilized in any form or by any means without written permission from the publisher.

Apex is distributed by North Star Editions:
sales@northstareditions.com | 888-417-0195

Produced for Apex by Red Line Editorial.

Photographs ©: Gareth Fuller/PA Wire/AP Images, cover, 24; Michel Spingler/AP Images, 1, 8, 22–23, 26, 27; Shutterstock Images, 4–5, 6, 6–7, 9, 10–11, 15, 18, 29; Wikimedia Commons, 12; David Caulkin/AP Images, 14; Jacques Langevin/Sygma/Getty Images, 16–17; PA/PA Wire/AP Images, 20; AP Images, 21; Frank Augstein/AP Images, 25

Library of Congress Control Number: 2023910841

ISBN
978-1-63738-747-4 (hardcover)
978-1-63738-790-0 (paperback)
978-1-63738-874-7 (ebook pdf)
978-1-63738-833-4 (hosted ebook)

Printed in the United States of America
Mankato, MN
012024

NOTE TO PARENTS AND EDUCATORS

Apex books are designed to build literacy skills in striving readers. Exciting, high-interest content attracts and holds readers' attention. The text is carefully leveled to allow students to achieve success quickly. Additional features, such as bolded glossary words for difficult terms, help build comprehension.

TABLE OF CONTENTS

CHAPTER 1
Road Trip 4

CHAPTER 2
Crossing the Channel 10

CHAPTER 3
Construction 16

CHAPTER 4
A Big Difference 22

COMPREHENSION QUESTIONS • 28
GLOSSARY • 30
TO LEARN MORE • 31
ABOUT THE AUTHOR • 31
INDEX • 32

CHAPTER 1

ROAD TRIP

A group of friends wants to drive across Europe. They live in England. So, they will have to cross the English **Channel**.

The English Channel is a body of water between England and France.

By the late 2010s, trains carried 7,300 cars through the tunnel every day.

The friends drive down a ramp. Then, they pull into a large train car. The train carries **vehicles** through the Channel Tunnel.

CARS, BIKES, AND TRAINS

Driving, biking, and walking through the tunnel are not allowed. People can drive cars onto trains. People with bicycles get on a bus. Then a train takes the bus through.

Passengers with no cars can ride Eurostar trains.

The train zooms through the tunnel. The journey takes just 35 minutes. Now, the friends can explore France.

Trains crossing the channel can go up to 100 miles per hour (160 km/h).

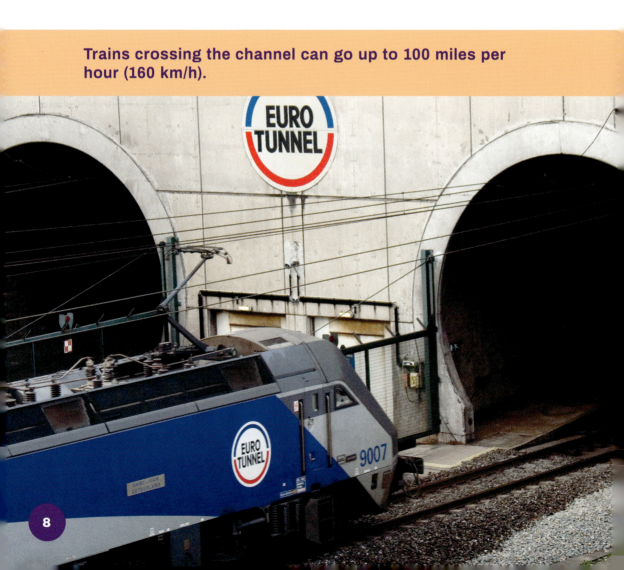

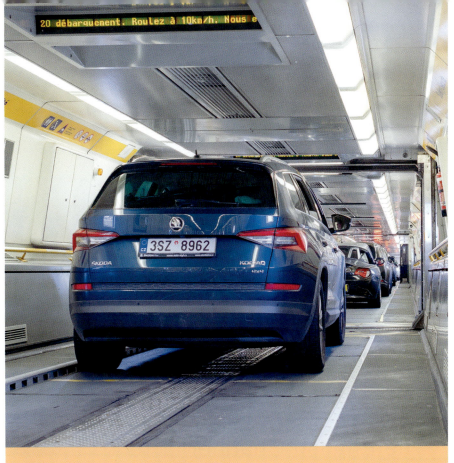

One train can hold 120 cars.

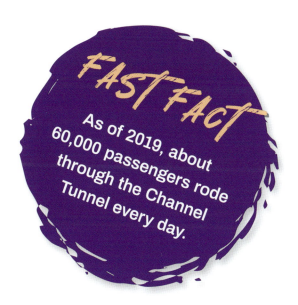

FAST FACT

As of 2019, about 60,000 passengers rode through the Channel Tunnel every day.

CHAPTER 2

CROSSING THE CHANNEL

The English Channel is part of the Atlantic Ocean. England is on one side. The rest of Europe is on the other. For years, only boats or planes could cross.

Some people still ride across the English Channel on boats.

People wanted a faster way across the English Channel. So, England and France worked together. They decided to build a tunnel.

OTHER IDEAS

People had long thought about ways to cross the channel. They even made plans in the 1800s. One plan was for a road bridge. But all those plans fell apart.

In the 1800s, people wanted to make a tunnel for horse-drawn carriages.

In 1986, leaders in France and England signed a treaty that allowed the tunnel to be built.

The Channel Tunnel was designed with three tunnels. Two would be for trains. One would be for service and security.

FAST FACT

The tunnel crosses the Strait of Dover. It's the narrowest part of the English Channel.

Parts of the English Channel are only 21 miles (33 km) wide.

The Strait of Dover

CHAPTER 3

CONSTRUCTION

Digging began in 1987. It started on the English side. The next year, digging began in France. Workers made sure both sides would meet. They used lasers to do this.

Workers dug a giant well on the shore.

Workers used tunnel **boring** machines (TBMs). These machines dug through the ground. Then, the machines used **conveyor belts**. The belts moved the **debris** back.

BIG MACHINES
The TBMs for the Channel Tunnel were powerful. They were up to 29 feet (9 m) wide. They could drill 250 feet (76 m) in one day.

◀ Tunnel boring machines can be more than 50 feet (15 m) wide.

Next, workers lined the tunnel walls. They covered it with iron and concrete. This made the tunnel extra strong.

Workers met in the middle of the English Channel on December 1, 1990.

It cost more than $20 billion to build the Channel Tunnel.

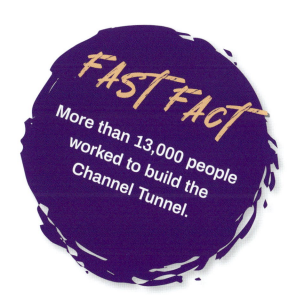

FAST FACT

More than 13,000 people worked to build the Channel Tunnel.

CHAPTER 4

A Big Difference

The Channel Tunnel opened in 1994. Trains began carrying passengers between England and France. They also carried vehicles and **cargo**.

Trains travel more than 31 miles (50 km) through the Channel Tunnel.

About 4,600 trucks go through the tunnel every day.

The tunnel changed the way people traveled. A **ferry** from England to France took 90 minutes. A train ride through the Channel Tunnel only took 35 minutes.

TRUCKS

The tunnel also changed business. Companies could carry cargo faster. In 2021, more than 1,600 **freight** trains used the tunnel. And more than 1.4 million trucks went through.

Some train cars are built to carry large trucks

The Channel Tunnel has the longest underwater section of any tunnel in the world. It stays underwater for 23.5 miles (37.8 km).

Workers help keep the Channel Tunnel open.

The tunnel is open 24 hours a day. It stays open every day of the year.

FAST FACT

In the 2010s, about 500 trains traveled through the tunnel each day.

COMPREHENSION QUESTIONS

Write your answers on a separate piece of paper.

1. Write a few sentences describing the main ideas of Chapter 2.

2. Would you rather go through the Channel Tunnel or across the English Channel in a boat? Why?

3. In what year did workers begin digging the Channel Tunnel?
    - **A.** 1987
    - **B.** 1994
    - **C.** 2021

4. How much faster is it to take a train across the English Channel than a ferry?
    - **A.** 35 minutes
    - **B.** 55 minutes
    - **C.** 90 minutes

5. What does **strait** mean in this book?

*The tunnel crosses the **Strait** of Dover. It's the narrowest part of the English Channel.*

    A. a very large ocean
    B. a thin body of water
    C. a small town or village

6. What does **zooms** mean in this book?

*The train **zooms** through the tunnel. The journey takes just 35 minutes.*

    A. is very loud
    B. stops inside
    C. goes quickly

Answer key on page 32.

GLOSSARY

boring
Making a hole, often by using some kind of drill.

cargo
Items carried by a plane, ship, train, or truck from one place to another.

channel
A length of water that joins two larger areas of water and is wider than a strait.

conveyor belts
Bands of fabric or rubber that move objects from one place to another.

debris
Pieces of something that broke or fell apart.

ferry
A boat that transports people and cars across water.

freight
Large amounts of goods carried by ships, trains, or trucks.

vehicles
Things like ships, cars, and trains that people can ride in.

TO LEARN MORE

BOOKS

Jackson, Tom. *Oresund Bridge and Other Great Building Feats*. Minneapolis: Lerner Publications, 2024.

Light, Kate. *20 Fun Facts About Famous Tunnels*. New York: Gareth Stevens Publishing, 2020.

Rossiter, Brienna. *World's Fastest Trains*. Mendota Heights, MN: Apex Editions, 2022.

ONLINE RESOURCES

Visit **www.apexeditions.com** to find links and resources related to this title.

ABOUT THE AUTHOR

Ashley Gish has authored many juvenile nonfiction books. She enjoys learning and sharing information with others. Ashley lives in southern Minnesota with her family.

A
Atlantic Ocean, 10

C
cargo, 22, 25
cars, 7

E
England, 4, 10, 13, 16, 22, 24
English Channel, 4, 10, 13, 15

F
France, 8, 13, 16, 22, 24

L
lasers, 16

P
passengers, 9, 22

S
Strait of Dover, 15

T
trains, 6–8, 14, 22, 25, 27
trucks, 25
tunnel boring machines (TBMs), 19

W
walls, 20

ANSWER KEY:
1. Answers will vary; 2. Answers will vary; 3. A; 4. B; 5. B; 6. C